W9-CHW-315

YO-YO MAGIC

David Oliver

BARNES
&NOBLE
BOOKS
NEW YORK

This edition published by
Barnes & Noble, Inc.,
by arrangement with Mars Publishing

1999 Barnes & Noble Books

M 10 9 8 7 6 5 4 3 2 1

ISBN: 0-7607-1632-3

Edited, designed and produced by Haldane Mason, London

Editorial Director: Sydney Francis
Art Director: Ron Samuel
Editor: Jane Ellis
Design: Zoë Mellors
Illustrations: Stephen Dew

Printed in China

CAUTION
Yo-yos are not suitable for children under three years old. Young children should not
be allowed to play with the yo-yo unsupervised.

Contents

History of the Yo-yo	4
Setting Up	6
Maintenance	8

The Spinner	10	The Elevator	27
The Slapper	11	The Third Dimension	28
Outward Bound	12	Pinwheels	30
Around the World	14	Shoot for the Moon	31
Hop the Fence	16	Flying Saucer	32
Walk the Dog	18	Skin the Cat	34
The Creeper	19	Dragster	36
Robin Hood	20	Sky Rocket	37
Motorbike	21	Breakaway	38
Rock the Baby	22	Tightrope	39
Loops	24	Into Orbit	40
Three Leaf-Clover	25	Double Skin the Cat	42
The Monkey	26	Barrel Rolls	44

Suppliers	46
Index	48

History of the Yo-yo

There are a number of stories surrounding the origins of the yo-yo. Perhaps the most popular is that ancient stone yo-yos were used as hunting weapons by warriors in the Philippines. However, this now appears unlikely, and the latest evidence shows the yo-yo appearing first in Greece around 500 B.C. Made from wood, metal or clay, these early yo-yos appear to have been popular toys in the cradle of civilization.

From there the yo-yo spread across the ancient world, changing little over the centuries. Much later, the toy became popular among the aristocracy of eighteenth-century France where it was known as un emigrette or joujou de Normandie. The craze spread throughout France, filtering down from the upper classes until everyone was at it. There is even evidence that Napoleon's troops played with their emigrettes before the battle of Waterloo. The craze spread to England. After a picture of the Prince of Wales playing with his bandalore (as it was then called) was produced, everyone with any idea of fashion had to own one. Later, during the days of the British Empire, the bandalore spread around the world.

However, the yo-yo as we know it today probably appeared first in the Philippines where yo-yoing caught on to such an extent that it became a national pastime. The big difference with Filipino yo-yos was that the string was not tied to the axle, but instead looped around it, allowing spinning tricks to be performed. This was the turning point that changed yo-yoing from a basic toy into a sport with virtually limitless possibilities for tricks. It was also in the Philippines that the toy first became known as the yo-yo – the Filipino word for "come-come" or "to return."

An American entrepreneur in the 1920s was so impressed by the skill of the local people with their hand-carved wooden yo-yos that he started a company making yo-yos based on the Filipino design. Donald Duncan was the man who turned the yo-yo into a worldwide sensation. He had a team of "Duncan yo-yo professionals" who toured the United States and Europe, demonstrating tricks and generally creating a demand for this exciting "new" toy. Because he had trademarked the word yo-yo, other companies that tried to cash in on the toy's success were forced to call their creations by other names. "Whirl-a-gig" and "returning top" were popular toys, but didn't have the appeal of the original. It wasn't until 1965 that courts in the United States ordered that the word yo-yo couldn't be used as a trademark, as it had become a permanent part of the language.

Since the 1970s, technology has improved the yo-yo greatly from its humble beginnings as a single piece of carved wood with a string attached. Weighting the outside edge of the yo-yo helped it to spin longer. In 1978 the first "take-apart" yo-yo with a replaceable axle was produced; 1980 saw the first yo-yo with "a brain," a special gear that helped the yo-yo to return to the hand. In the 1990s came ball-bearing axles that increased spin times even more.

The yo-yo you receive with Yo-yo Magic won't set any records, but it will certainly get you started and set you on the road to discovering the secrets of the yo-yo. Who knows, you might even have something to contribute to the long and varied history of this greatest of toys.

Setting Up

String length

Make sure your yo-yo string is the right length for you.

Hold the end of the string and let the yo-yo hang at the end of it, just touching the ground. Rest the palm of your hand on your stomach, with the lower edge touching your navel. Where the string touches the higher edge of your palm is the length your string should be.

If the string is too long, tie a loop in the string at this point and then cut off the excess string with a pair of scissors.

It's important to make sure your string is the right length for you. Too many people are deterred because their first yo-yo wasn't set up properly. The yo-yo should reach the end of the string above the ground without your having to raise your arm too high or too low.

The loop

*P*ass part of the string through the loop to create another loop.

Place the loop over your middle finger, between the first and second knuckle. Don't forget to loosen the loop from time to time, so that your finger doesn't get sore.

The throw

*H*old your yo-yo in front of you with your arm bent. Your palm should be facing towards you, and the string should be running from your finger above the yo-yo. Move your hand forward and down, and flick your wrist downward, releasing the yo-yo to drop toward the ground. The quicker you flick, the more force you will give to the yo-yo and the more control you will have over it.

Turn your hand over, palm open, and just before the yo-yo reaches the end of the string, gently lift your hand upward.

Get it right, and the yo-yo will return to your waiting hand.

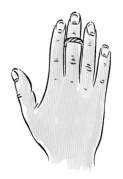

Maintenance

The string

1 Your string should give you a good week's yo-yoing. If it starts to appear worn or dirty, get another one.

2 Worn yo-yo strings can be dangerous – change your string often.

Spare strings can be bought in many toy stores.

3 To replace your string, unwind the end of the string until you can fit it over the yo-yo.

4 How tightly the string is wrapped around the axle of the yo-yo will affect the kind of tricks you can do.

Tight
If the string is tight, it's better for throwing loops.

Loose
If it's loose, it's better for spinner tricks.

Double loop
With some yo-yos, you may need to twist the string and put it around again to form a double loop. See what works best for you.

The Spinner

1 Throw the yo-yo in the usual way.

2 Instead of lifting your arm to bring the yo-yo back up the string, let your arm stay in the same position as when the yo-yo left your hand.

3 The yo-yo should spin at the bottom of the string. While it does so, turn your hand over so your palm is facing downward.

4 Tug sharply to bring the yo-yo back to your hand.

The Slapper

1 Throw a spinner.

2 When you're ready to bring the yo-yo back up the string, slap the back of your yo-yo hand. The yo-yo will immediately return up the string. This trick is very simple, but impressive.

Outward Bound

Tip
This trick looks sensational, but it is actually easy to do. Once you become good at it, you can experiment by throwing the yo-yo from behind your back, or under your leg, or you can even use two yo-yos.

1 Hold your hand by your side, palm facing behind you.

2 Raise your arm firmly upward and outward and release the yo-yo when your arm is straight out in front of you. You'll need a good snap of the wrist to get enough power to the yo-yo.

3 When the yo-yo reaches the end of the string, it should hang for a split second.

4 Then it will return. Be sure to catch it palm up.

Tip
This trick needs a lot of power, so be careful when the yo-yo comes back – it might be going faster than you thought!

Around the World

1 Throw an outward bound.

2 As the yo-yo reaches the end of the string, lift your arm up and over.

3 The yo-yo will spin at the end of the string and go around you in a full circle.

4 When the yo-yo is back in front of you, give it a sharp tug and it will return to your hand.

5 You can go around the world more than once — see how many trips you can make.

Hop the Fence

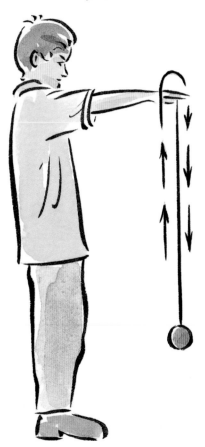

1 Make a basic throw, and turn your palm face down in the usual way, as if you are going to catch the yo-yo on its return.

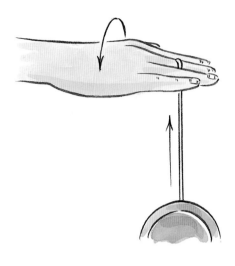

2 As the yo-yo comes back up the string, instead of catching it, flick your hand over so your palm is facing upward.

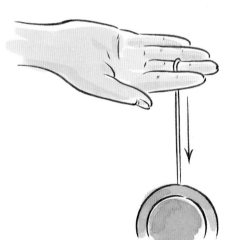

3 The yo-yo will flip over your hand and head back toward the floor.

4 Catch your yo-yo on the way back up – or make it hop the fence again.

Walk the Dog

1 Throw a fast spinner.

2 Lower the spinning yo-yo gently to the floor.

3 The yo-yo should run along the ground in front of you.

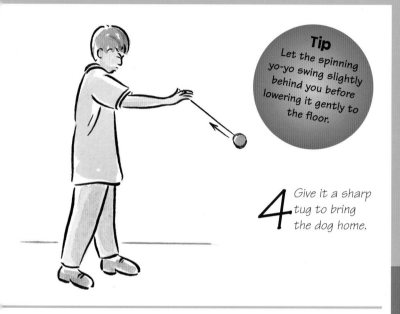

Tip
Let the spinning yo-yo swing slightly behind you before lowering it gently to the floor.

4 Give it a sharp tug to bring the dog home.

The Creeper

1 While your dog is out for his stroll, lower your hand to just above the ground.

2 Give the string a sharp tug and the little fellow will come creeping back.

Robin Hood

1 Throw a spinner.

2 Grab the string just below your finger and pull it over your thumb, like a bow.

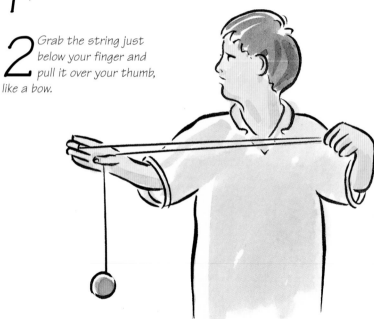

3 When the yo-yo is a few inches below your hand, let go of the string.

4 The yo-yo will snap back into your hand.

Motorbike

This trick is easy to do and will show everyone nearby that you are a yo-yo champ.

1 Throw a fast spinner.

2 Gently lower the yo-yo up and down on a hard surface.

3 You'll hear the yo-yo revving up like a motorbike!

Rock the Baby

1 Throw a spinner.

2 Grab the string about halfway down with your other hand.

3 Grab it again a few inches above the spinning yo-yo with your throwing hand.

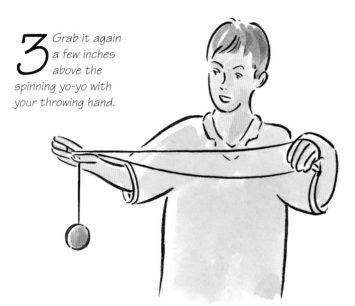

4 Move your free hand down and stretch your fingers out so the string forms a triangle. Rock the baby back and forth a few times before letting go and snapping the yo-yo back to your hand.

Loops

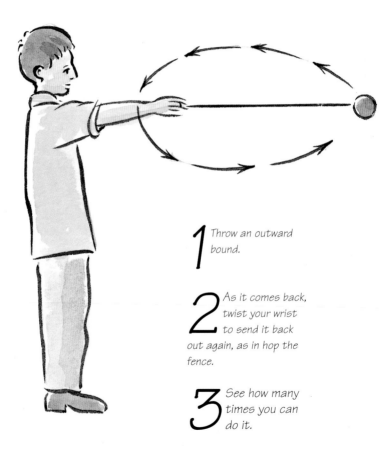

1 Throw an outward bound.

2 As it comes back, twist your wrist to send it back out again, as in hop the fence.

3 See how many times you can do it.

Three-Leaf Clover

1 Throw an outward bound straight up in the air.

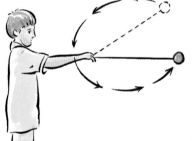

2 Bring it into a loop, then send it out again straight in front of you.

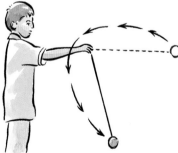

3 When it comes back again, send it straight down toward the ground.

The Monkey

This trick is great fun and it is also the basis for the elevator.

1 Throw a fast spinner.

2 Place the index finger of your free hand about halfway down the string.

3 Place your throwing hand level with your other about 12 inches (30 centimeters) to the side.

4 The monkey will climb the string.

The Elevator

1 Do the monkey, but instead of moving your yo-yo hand forward, bring it down and thread the string through the groove of the yo-yo.

2 Move your yo-yo hand up and down and watch the elevator rise and fall.

The Third Dimension

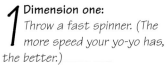

1 **Dimension one:**
Throw a fast spinner. (The more speed your yo-yo has, the better.)

2 **Dimension two:**
Grab the string just below your yo-yo hand and pull it across your thumb until the yo-yo is about 6 inches (15 centimeters) below your right hand. Now you've gone from the first dimension (up and down) to the second (left and right).

3 **Dimension three:**
Swing the yo-yo out and over in a miniature around the world. This is the third dimension (back and forth).

4 **The finish:**
Let go of the string. When the string straightens, give the yo-yo a sharp tug to bring it back to your hand.

Pinwheels

1 Throw a spinner.

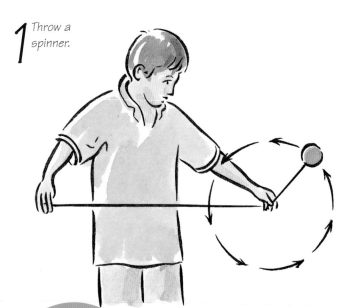

Tip
Make sure the yo-yo doesn't turn on its side or you will lose the momentum of the spin and not be able to bring the yo-yo back up the string.

2 Grab the string a few inches from the yo-yo and swing it in a circle.

Shoot for the Moon

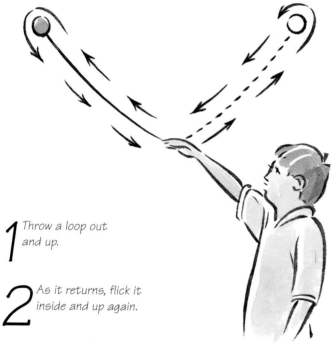

1 Throw a loop out and up.

2 As it returns, flick it inside and up again.

3 When it returns, either catch it or repeat it. This trick looks great if you can do it a few times in a row.

Flying Saucer

This is a trick especially for those of you who are interested in the extra-terrestrial!

1 Throw a spinner across your body.

2 The yo-yo should go into a spin on its side.

3 Grab the string a few inches from the yo-yo and lift it into the air.

4 When the yo-yo is level with your yo-yo hand, let go. The flying saucer should return to its home planet.

Skin the Cat

1 Throw a fast spinner.

2 Run the string over your finger and pull down so the cat climbs toward your hand.

3 As Puss approaches
your hand, give her a tug
so she jumps up and
over into an outward bound.

Dragster

Tip
To make it easier to get the string off your finger, put the loop around the first joint of your finger, rather than around the second joint, as normal.

1 Throw a fast spinner.

2 Take the string off your finger and drop the yo-yo to the ground. It will take off like a dragster, wrapping the string around itself as it goes.

Sky Rocket

This trick is like the dragster, but in a different dimension. Be careful with this one.

1 Throw a fast spinner.

2 Slip the string off your finger and give it a sharp tug into the air.

3 Let go of the string and the rocket will fly into orbit.

4 For full NASA membership, catch the rocket in your pocket on reentry.

Breakaway

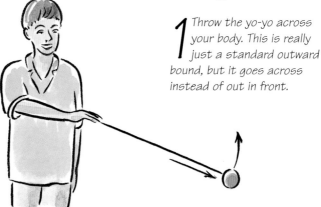

1 Throw the yo-yo across your body. This is really just a standard outward bound, but it goes across instead of out in front.

2 When the yo-yo reaches the end of the string, it should loop slightly upward and then return to your hand. This is a useful trick since it is the basis for all the tightrope tricks.

Tightrope

1 Throw a
spinner across
your body.

2 As it comes back,
put your finger
against the string
a few inches from
the yo-yo.

4 Allow the tightrope
walker to go back and
forth on the string
before tossing him into the air
to finish.

3 The yo-yo should hop
over your finger and on
to the string.

Tip
The closer you
put your finger
to the yo-yo, the
easier it is to get the
man onto the
tightrope.

Into Orbit

1 Throw a spinner.

3 Then give it a flick to bring it over your shoulder and down in front of you.

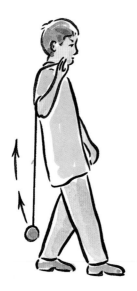

2 Hang the string over your shoulder.

4 **Variations:** It looks great if you give the yo-yo a kick with the back of your heel to bring it back.

5 You don't have to do this trick with your shoulder – you can drape the string over your outstretched arm, leg, or even your neck!

Double Skin the Cat

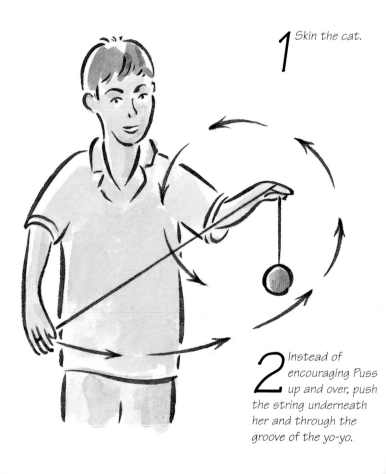

1 Skin the cat.

2 Instead of encouraging Puss up and over, push the string underneath her and through the groove of the yo-yo.

3 Now swing her around twice.

4 Finish with an outward bound or whatever takes your fancy.

Barrel Rolls

1 Throw a spinner.

2 As it reaches the end of the string, push the index finger of your free hand into the string just above the yo-yo, causing it to flip up. Then you bring your yo-yo hand down and your other hand up, so the yo-yo sits on the string, a bit like the tightrope.

3 Bring your hands together to create a loop. Put the index finger of your yo-yo hand into the loop between the yo-yo and the index finger of your other hand.

4 Move your hands in a pedaling motion to bring the yo-yo forward and round. Keep this up for as long as you can.

Suppliers

Many toy stores now supply yo-yos. Those listed below can offer advice and most run yo-yo competitions.

UK Stores

Air Time
Exeter: 01392 427776

Anti Gravity
York: 01904 631696

Barry Island Rollerdome
Barry Island: 01446 720808

Core Boards
Leicester: 0116 251 6167

Cunning Stunts
Salisbury: 01722 410588

Fuzzy Navel
Wakefield: 01924 366400

High Jinx
Gloucester: 01452 503 412

Kaos
Worcester: 01905 611820

Kreative Kites
Newbury: 01635 528400

Ocean Kites
Southampton: 01703 334222

Off The Edge
Macclesfield: 01625 613008

Perpetual Motion
Sheffield: 0114 266 0321

Route One
Oxford: 01865 246887
Bath: 01225 446 710
Guildford: 01483 570688
Kingston Upon Thames: 0181 546 5766
Brighton: 01273 323633
Cardiff: 01222 666485
Cheltenham: 01242 255411
Tunbridge Wells: 0189 253 9599

Street Blades
Swansea: 01792 464545

The Toy Station
Richmond Upon Thames: 0181 940 4896

UFO
Weston Super Mare: 01934 644988

Whaam
Grays, Thurrock: 01708 864074
Chelmsford: 01245 359252

Yo! Station
Chester: 01244 312136

US Manufacturers

The Duke of Whirl

PO Box 44393, Phoenix, AZ 85064

e-mail: dukewhirl@aol.com

Spintastics Skill Toys, Inc.

3121 Birch Ave., Grapevine,

TX 76051,

817-318-7746

e-mail: spintastics@spintastics.com

SuperYo

PO Box 1707, Bothell, WA 98041-1707,

USA (888) 249-YOYO (9696)

fax: (425) 712-9696

e-mail: sales@superyo.com

Wallace Toy Company

Box 349, Wallace, Idaho USA 83873

What's Next Manufacturers, Inc.

PO Box 276, Arcade, New York 14009

phone: (716) 492-1014

Wooden Monarch Yo-yos

PO Box 23404, Santa Barbara,

CA USA 93121

phone: (805) 966-4270

e-mail: mreid@rain.org

Yomega Corp.-YR

Retail Dept. PO Box 4146, Fall River,

MA USA 02723-0402

phone: (800) 338-8796

Yo-yos on the Net

Yo UK

www.yo-yo.co.uk

This British site offers good
contacts around the country,
competitions and info on yo-yos.

Cosmic yo-yos

http://www.iwc.com/cosmicyo/

Good advice, yo-yo reviews and loads
of tricks on this American site.

Just say yo!

http://www.socool.com/socool/yo-
yo.html

American website with plenty of
contacts and links.

Tomer's page of exotic yo-yo

http://pages.nyu.edu/~tqm3413/yoyo/

One of the best sites on the Web
for tricks.

Yo-yo in Ireland

http://www.infj.ulst.ac.uk/~czwq22/yo
yo.html

Good links and tips on this Irish-
based site.

Index

A

Around the world,	14–15
Axles,	5, 9

B

Ball-bearing axles,	5
Bandalore,	4
Barrel rolls,	44–5
"Brain",	5
Breakaway,	38
British Empire,	4

C

Clover, three-leaf,	25
The creeper,	19

D

Double skin the cat,	42–3
Dragster,	36
Duncan, Donald,	5

E

The elevator,	27

F

Flying saucer,	32–3
France,	4

H

History,	4–5
Hop the fence,	16–17

I

Into orbit,	40–1

L

Loops:	
double loops,	9
setting up,	7
tricks,	24

M

Maintenance,	8–9
The monkey,	26
Motorbike,	21

O

Outward bound,	12–13

P

Philippines,	4–5
Pinwheels,	30

R

Robin Hood,	20
Rock the baby,	22–3

S

Setting up,	6–7
Shoot for the moon,	31
Skin the cat,	34–5
double,	42–3
Sky rocket,	37
The slapper,	11
The spinner,	10–11
String:	
length,	6
loops,	7, 9
maintenance,	8–9
Suppliers,	46–7

T

The third dimension,	28–9
Three-leaf clover,	25
Throw,	7
Tightrope,	39

U

United States of America,	5

W

Walk the dog,	18–19